THE MOTHERS AND DAUGHTERS OF THE BIBLE

Speak

WORKBOOK

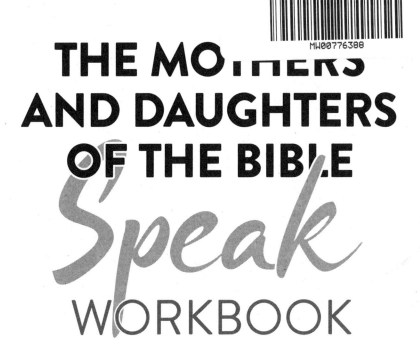

LESSONS ON FAITH
FROM
NINE BIBLICAL FAMILIES

SHANNON BREAM

HarperChristian
Resources

The Mothers and Daughters of the Bible Speak Workbook

© 2022 by Fox News Network LLC

Requests for information should be addressed to:

HarperChristian Resources, 3900 Sparks Dr. SE, Grand Rapids, Michigan 49546

ISBN 978–0–310–15597-3 (softcover)

ISBN 978-0–310-15598-0 (ebook)

All Scripture quotations are taken from the Holy Bible, New International Version®, NIV®. Copyright © 1973, 1978, 1984, 2011 by Biblica, Inc.® Used by permission. All rights reserved worldwide. www.Zondervan.com. The "NIV" and "New International Version" are trademarks registered in the United States Patent and Trademark Office by Biblica, Inc.®

Any internet addresses (websites, blogs, etc.) and telephone numbers in this study guide are offered as a resource. They are not intended in any way to be or imply an endorsement by HarperChristian Resources, nor does HarperChristian Resources vouch for the content of these sites and numbers for the life of this study guide.

HarperChristian Resources titles may be purchased in bulk for church, business, fundraising, or ministry use. For information, please e-mail ResourceSpecialist@ChurchSource.com.

First Printing November 2022 / Printed in the United States of America

Contents

Welcome

Mothers are the first protectors as infants prepare to enter the world. Many of them pray over their children long before they have a name, storing up hopes and dreams for their little ones. As their children grow, daughters (and sons), often chart their own courses. Sometimes this brings great joy, other times great sorrow. This isn't just true of earthly mothers and daughters, but those we consider our spiritual mothers and daughters, too.

God uses mothers and daughters in critical roles throughout the Old and New Testaments. They're often used to change the course of history and reveal the depths of His love.

In the upcoming pages, you'll explore the stories of women and their family dynamics throughout the Bible. You'll find that these aren't just characters from a book. They're genuine, authentic people who celebrated and mourned, took great risks, and received remarkable rewards. They shed heavy tears and grieved just like you.

They faced many of the same difficulties we face today: battles with infertility, difficult relational dynamics, severe family rejection. They, too, knew disappointment, heartache, and loneliness. Yet these mothers and daughters turned to God as their protector and provider.

And the same God who worked mightily in their lives is at work in yours, too. May you find comfort and hope as we make this journey together.

* * *

How to Use
This Workbook

This workbook follows #1 *New York Times* bestseller, *The Mothers and Daughters of the Bible Speak*, and it's designed to make your experience richer and deeper. In the upcoming nine lessons, you'll be challenged to consider the parallels between each mother and daughter story and your own. You'll be asked to reflect on how God worked in their lives and how He's working in yours, too.

If you join with friends or neighbors to complete this workbook, consider answering the questions personally *before* you meet up. That way you'll be the most prepared with insights, reflections, and thoughts to share.

You'll notice that each lesson has four components:

*R*EFLECT invites you to read key moments of each woman's life in the Bible and connect with her story.

*C*ONNECT asks you to consider how God in the Old Testament or Jesus in the New Testament responds to each woman and what this discloses about His character and how He responds to you.

*R*EVEAL provides an opportunity to identify how God works through the woman's relationship, responses to God, and acts of faith, as well as your similar relationships, responses, and acts of faith.

*P*RAY asks you to prayerfully consider the woman's story and how her relationship ties into the work God is doing in your life right now.

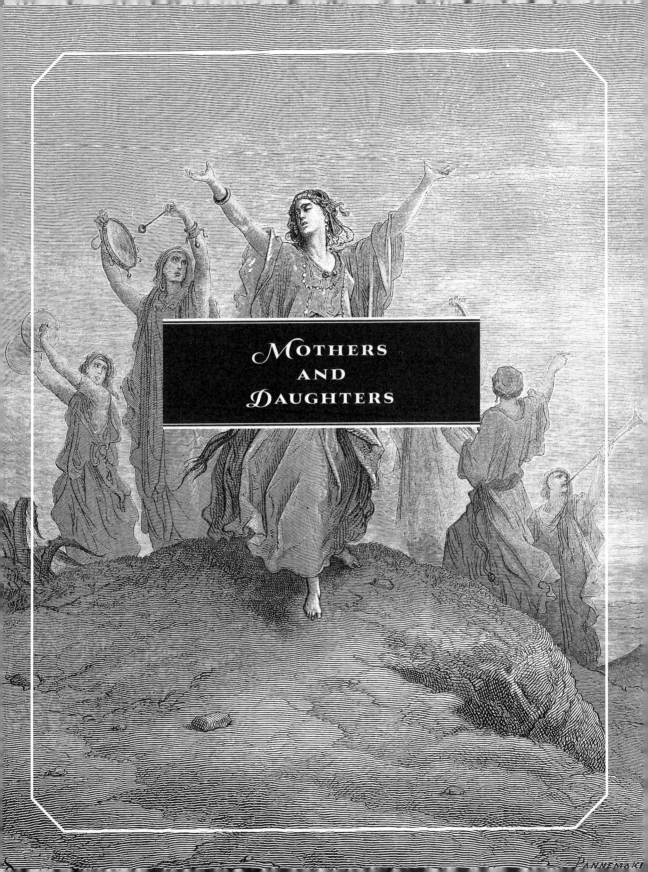

MOTHERS
AND
DAUGHTERS

JOCHEBED AND MIRIAM

Jochebed and Miriam—it's through the bravery and sacrifice of this mother and daughter that the entire story of Scripture begins to unfold. What a gift God gives us in the biblical account marked by the faith, creativity, and courage of these two women!

—From *The Mothers and Daughters of the Bible Speak*, page 6

From Eve to Sarah to Rebekah to Rachel and Leah, motherhood plays a key role in the early stories of the Bible. But we rarely see these mothers interacting with their children—and of the mothers who are named in Genesis, Leah is the only one whom the Bible mentions as having a daughter. In Exodus, we see the first mother and daughter pair interacting with each other in Scripture—Jochebed and Miriam.

REFLECT

In Genesis 37, we're introduced to Joseph, one of the great heroes of the Bible. Joseph is sold into slavery by his brothers and launches into an adventure filled with surprise twists and turns. God positions Joseph to save his entire family and his people during a severe famine. The Jewish people flourish in Egypt for years, until a new Pharoah takes control of the land and enslaves God's people. Pharoah becomes so paranoid and fearful of the success and power of God's people that he commands a genocide. Every male newborn from a Hebrew family must be thrown into the Nile River and drown to death.

Jochebed gives birth to Miriam and raises her according to Hebrew custom. Then she becomes pregnant again. The stakes couldn't have been higher. Take a moment. Imagine yourself as a Hebrew mother, counting down the days until the child's birth. If you give birth to a girl, the child will live in slavery; but if it's a boy, the child will be slaughtered. Pharaoh and his cruel decree didn't just create a genocide, it stole the joy of motherhood.

Read Exodus 2:1–2. What divine insight does God give Jochebed as she looks at her child?

Read the following passages. What does each one affirm about the specialness that Jochebed sees?

Acts 7:20

Hebrews 11:23

When have you recognized something special or been given divine insight about a child at a young age?

How did this affect the way you watched or protected the child?

This mother was courageous and crafty. When she realized she could no longer conceal Moses, Jochebed coated a basket with tar and pitch, essentially making a baby ark for him. She made a plan and used the resources she had. Jochebed placed the basket among the reeds on the bank of the Nile River—the very place she'd been commanded to send her baby to die. She knew Moses had a special destiny, so to give him a chance at that life, Jochebed let her infant son go. The word for this basket is the same used to describe Noah's ark in Genesis 6.

—From *The Mothers and Daughters of the Bible Speak*, pages 15–16

When someone is first introduced in the Bible, it's important to pay attention to how the person is described and their initial actions. This often alludes to characteristics, challenges, or roles he or she will have as the stories unfold.

Read Exodus 2:3–4. How is Moses' big sister, Miriam, introduced in this passage?

What characteristics does she display?

Read Exodus 2:5–9. How does Miriam leverage the kindness of Pharoah's daughter to save her brother?

The Pharoah had issued a decree for the Hebrew sons, yet God is at work in his daughter's heart. But Miriam doesn't know that! First, she steps forward and addresses Pharoah's daughter, a child putting herself squarely between her brother and one of the most powerful people in Egypt. She abandons the safety of her hiding spot. She could have stayed put in a hidden place, and then, when the coast was clear, run back to her mother to tell her the good news. That would have been a happy ending. But Miriam doesn't do that. Instead, she does another brave thing: She speaks up and offers a solution that will either expose her family's secret or buy them more time with this vulnerable baby.

Instead of being filled with coldness and cruelty like her father, Pharoah's daughter shows great compassion.

How do Miriam's courageous actions help keep the family together?

When have you done something risky or courageous to try to keep your immediate or spiritual family together?

What was the result?

Which of the following displays God's power and presence? Place a check (√) by all that apply.

_____ Jochebed determined to save her son despite the edict against his life.

_____ Miriam boldly stepped forward to protect her brother.

_____ Pharaoh's daughter took pity on the infant and spared his life.

Which is most meaningful to you today? Why?

How do you suspect God is positioning you as part of a spiritual mother/daughter team to advance God's will and way?

Read Exodus 2:10. What mixed emotions do you think Jochebed felt as her son was given to Pharoah's daughter?

When have you felt mixed emotions in trusting what you loved most to God?

Jochebed and Miriam were forced to stand by, pray, and trust that God was at work. Where is God currently asking you to stand by, pray, and trust He is at work?

Jochebed's life shows impact and eternal importance of motherhood—both physical and spiritual. The spiritual foundation she lays during her son's formative years would make all the difference decades later, when Moses struggles with and then ultimately follows God's calling on his life.

—From *The Mothers and Daughters of the Bible Speak*, page 18

The tragedy starts when Moses tries to become his people's savior too early. Somewhere during his years in Pharoah's household, Moses came to identify with his Hebrew brothers and sisters and the injustice and struggle they faced.

Read Exodus 2:11–15. What snap decision does Moses make?

How was Moses betrayed by the people he saw as his own?

What must Moses do and give up in order to survive?

How do you think Jochebed, his loving mother, and Miriam, his loving sister, mourned and grieved when they heard the news?

When have you mourned and grieved over your child or spiritual child's foolhardy decision?

What carried you, or is carrying you now, through that difficult season?

Moses wants to be a warrior savior, saving his people by his own strength. Like Joseph, he has to go through a period of suffering—a "wilderness" period—when he must rely on God and be transformed by God's presence, before he can be a liberator to his people.

Read Exodus 3:1–14. How does God reveal his presence to Moses and call him to a special mission?

In the space below, draw a picture of the burning bush scene.

List three burning-bush moments from your life and their outcomes.

❋ _____

❋ _____

❋ _____

How is this interaction between God and Moses an answer to the prayers of his mother, Jochebed, his entire family, and the Israelites?

On a scale of one to ten, how much do you believe in the power of prayer? (Circle) where you land on the spectrum.

— ❶ — ❷ — ❸ — ❹ — ❺ — ❻ — ❼ — ❽ — ❾ — ⑩ —

What prevents you from having a more consistent prayer life?

Despite this powerful encounter with God, Moses still second-guessed himself. Read Exodus 4:10–16. How is Jochebed's son, Aaron, partnered and positioned with Moses to set Israel free?

How do you think Jochebed, as a mother, responded emotionally and spiritually to watching her sons, Moses and Aaron, confront Pharoah repeatedly?

Read Exodus 14:15–29. After a series of miraculous signs, God's people are freed from the cruelties of Pharoah. All too soon, they find themselves pinned up against the Red Sea, the Egyptian army in hot pursuit. God opens the Red Sea revealing dry ground. God's people cross safely to the opposite shore. Then in a fit of confusion and rage, the army and all their chariots are destroyed by the crashing waters. That's when we see the trio of siblings united in exuberant joy.

Read Exodus 15:19–21. How does Miriam demonstrate her leadership and passionate worship?

Despite all odds, all three of Jochebed's children become mighty leaders of Israel. Miriam becomes a prophetess and leader. Aaron becomes the founder of Israel's priesthood. And Moses leads God's people to victory.

Jochebed models faith for us. She was a woman so in tune with God that she was able to see an extraordinary vision for her son. That trust in God gave her the holy courage to defy an evil king's murderous order. She used what she had and released her precious baby to God's plan. It can be tough for us to surrender our loved ones to God, and Jochebed did it more than once.

Which of your loved ones are you struggling to surrender to God?

Who are three immediate and spiritual children for whom you pray regularly?

✿ _____

✿ _____

✿ _____

For what do you specifically ask God?

✿ _____

✿ _____

✿ _____

How does Jochebed's story challenge and encourage you to keep praying and trusting God with your loved ones?

$\mathcal{C}$ONNECT

Now that you've read and reflected on Jochebed's story alongside her children— Miriam, Moses, and Aaron—it's time to connect this mother and her children of the Bible with your life. Fill out the chart below.

What do you see as Jochebed's greatest character strengths as a mother?	
What do you see as Jochebed's greatest struggles as a mother?	
Which strengths do you relate to or long for?	
Which struggles do you relate to or long to overcome?	
How do you hope to be more like Jochebed in your spiritual motherhood and faith journey?	

REVEAL

Now that you've connected with this mother in the Bible, it's time to look at how God reveals His character and faithfulness to Jochebed and how God is doing the same for you.

Where did you most see God show up in Jochebed's and her children's lives?	
What does God reveal about Himself and His character in the life of Jochebed?	
Like Jochebed, in what ways have you experienced God protecting you and your loved ones, and answering your prayers?	
How is God calling you to pray for them now?	

$\mathscr{P}$RAY

Take a few minutes to ask the Holy Spirit to guide you as you respond to the following prayer prompts.

Lord, like Jochebed, help me . . .

_____

_____

_____

Lord, where am I responding out of fear and panic rather than trust and prayer?

_____

_____

_____

Lord, here are the names of the loved ones about whom I'm most concerned. Will You reveal Your power and presence to each one? (Write the names below.)

_____

_____

_____

Lord, what can I do this week to encourage and bless these loved ones?

_____

_____

_____

Lord, considering Jochebed's story, how are You calling me to love and live differently?

_____

_____

_____

RUTH AND NAOMI

Again and again in Scripture, we see examples of "found families." Adoption is a theme God beautifully illustrates for us repeatedly in the Bible, leading up to the adoption of Christians as sons and daughters of God. . . . And, of course, Jesus' own story is one of adoption. He was known as the son of Joseph, but Joseph was His adoptive father—a man who took on a divine assignment that upended his life and called him to a challenging journey. . . . One of the most beautiful examples we get of a "chosen family" bond in the Old Testament is the relationship between Ruth and her mother-in-law, Naomi.

—From *The Mothers and Daughters of the Bible Speak,*
    pages 31–32

In *The Women of the Bible Speak*, we looked at Ruth's life in connection with Tamar—another woman who knew what it was to be an outcast and a stranger, someone people despised and perhaps pitied. Now we're going to see Ruth through the lens of being a daughter and the relationship she built with Naomi. Their journey begins in shared grief and results in deep joy and deliverance.

REFLECT

Naomi and her husband, Elimelek, leave their home country, Judah, during a famine, in search of a better life for themselves and their sons. They travel to Moab where the customs and traditions of the land couldn't be more different. Just as they begin building a new life, tragedy strikes. Nothing exacerbates grief and discomfort like being away from home—that which feels safe and familiar, surrounded by love.

Read Ruth 1:1–5. How does being in a foreign land exacerbate Naomi's grief?

When have you encountered loss, pain, or grief away from home?

Why does being away from home when hardship hits make it that much worse?

Naomi's situation becomes dire. In the ancient world, husbands and sons support the women of the family. When Naomi loses her spouse and children, she's impoverished. Then she finds a glimmer of hope. Back in her homeland of Judah, the famine has ended, and food is available.

Read Ruth 1:6–10. What hint do you see regarding Naomi's faith in verse 6?

In her grief and pain, how does Naomi selflessly respond to her daughters-in-law, Ruth and Orpah?

When you're facing grief and pain, are you more tempted to act selfishly or selflessly? Explain.

Naomi has a long, lonely, dangerous journey ahead of her. Yet she's willing to make the journey alone.

Read Ruth 1:11–13. Why is Naomi so concerned with Ruth and Orpah, as Moabites, staying in the land of Moab?

What could Ruth and Orpah lose by going with their mother-in-law Naomi?

Read Ruth 1:14–19. How does Ruth respond to her mother-in-law, Naomi?

What does this passage reveal about Ruth's and Orpah's special bond to Naomi?

The Bible often gives us examples of "found families." God uses the theme of adoption to illustrate the depths of His love—in people He brings together and in our adoption as sons and daughters of God.

Read Galatians 4:4–7 and Romans 8:15–17. What is the role of adoption in salvation?

What does the Bible reveal about the beauty of adoption through Ruth's and Naomi's story and these passages about adoption into the family of God?

The Hebrew word for daughter-in-law is *kallah* and it's a complicated word. It's sometimes translated as "bride," and it is used in that sense in the romantic imagery of the Song of Songs. But the root of the word *kallah* is *kalal*, which means "perfected" or "made complete." A daughter-in-law is not just a bride for the son, but she adds to the entire family unit. Naomi's daughters-in-law were her family, and for her to leave them behind in Moab would be to leave a part of her heart there as well.

—From *The Mothers and Daughters of the Bible Speak*, page 36

What do modern, negative stereotypes in culture suggest about mothers-in-law (examples: overbearing, nosy, hostile)?

How does this story challenge that narrative and demonstrate that mothers-in-law can be a gift and a blessing?

Though Naomi urges her to turn back, Ruth refuses. Many people look at this passage as an example of beautiful, earthly love, and they are right. But what about looking at the passage in another way—as a model for evangelism?

Naomi is the first person in this story to talk about the Lord, and that becomes a consistent theme in Naomi and Ruth's relationship. She reminds Ruth that going back home means going back to "her people and her gods" (Ruth 1:15), but Ruth persists. She wants to go with Naomi, and she wants to worship Naomi's God.

In the ancient Near East, religion was very closely linked to nationality and a people's culture. Ruth makes the decision to leave all that behind and align with the God of Naomi.

How are you living out your faith in a way that makes others want to believe in God?

Read Ruth 2:1–2. How does Ruth respond to Naomi?

What does Naomi calling Ruth "daughter" reveal about their relationship?

Who has been a second-mother or spiritual mother to you?

To whom have you been a second-mother or spiritual mother?

How has this relationship strengthened you emotionally, relationally, and spiritually?

Read Ruth 2:1–4. What do you notice about Boaz when he's first introduced in the Bible?

What do Boaz's first words reveal about his faith and love of God?

Read Ruth 2:5–10. As a man of faith, how does Boaz extend hospitality, kindness, and protection to Ruth?

What characterizes Ruth's response?

Read Ruth 2:11–16. How does Boaz live out his faith in this passage?

How are you living out your faith through the ways you treat and respond to others?

Read Leviticus 25:2–55. How does the Jewish law set up a system of accountability, so families are obligated to help their own, including distant relatives?

Read Ruth 2:17–20. How does Naomi respond to Boaz's kindness?

> Scripture talks a lot about the role of a "redeemer," and God Himself is often identified in the Old Testament as Redeemer—rescuer of the people of Israel. The Psalms refer to God as "my Rock and my Redeemer" (Psalm 19:14), and Job at the end of all his trials said, "I know that my redeemer lives, and that in the end he will stand on the earth" (Job 19:25). But when we talk about a redeemer in terms of the law—the kind of legal redeemer Boaz was—the context is one of obligation and responsibility.
>
> —From *The Mothers and Daughters of the Bible Speak*, page 46

What do Boaz's acts of kindness toward Ruth and Ruth's acts of kindness toward Naomi share in common?

How do Boaz and Ruth both act as redeemers?

Who is God calling you to join His work in writing a redemption story?

Read Titus 2:11–14. Who is the ultimate Redeemer?

How have you experienced the ultimate Redeemer in your life?

Naomi's maternal instincts on behalf of Ruth were strong. She sees a way forward for Ruth, the selfless daughter-in-law, who had abandoned her own hopes in order to protect Naomi.

Read Ruth 3:1–18. What does Naomi instruct Ruth to do and what's the result?

What does Ruth's obedience reveal about her relationship with Naomi?

With whom in your life could you develop this kind of relationship?

Read Ruth 4:1–12. Why does the first guardian-redeemer pass on buying the land from Naomi?

What risk does Boaz take by buying the land from Naomi?

What does Boaz's decision to buy the land and marry Ruth reveal about his character?

What do Boaz's generous, loving actions have in common with Jesus' loving actions for you?

When have you seen God provide for you in the most unlikely way?

Read Ruth 4:13–17. What sacrifice does Boaz make in taking Ruth to be his wife and in the birth of their son, Obed? Where is Obed in the lineage of Christ?

Naomi and Ruth, mother and daughter by choice, wind up with blessings beyond what they could have imagined.

How does Naomi's story demonstrate that God can work all things together for good and His glory?

How can you more intentionally engage with God's family—all the different kinds of mothers and daughters in your life—and build vibrant relationships?

ℭONNECT

Now that you've read and reflected on much of Naomi and her daughter-in-law's story, it's time to connect these women with your life. Fill out the chart below.

What do you see as Naomi's greatest character strengths as a mother-in-law? What do you see as Ruth's greatest character strengths as a daughter-in-law?	
What do you see as Naomi's and Ruth's greatest struggles in their relationship with each other and others?	
Which strengths do you relate to or long for?	
Which struggles do you relate to or long to overcome?	
How do you hope to be more like Naomi and Ruth in your familial or spiritual relationships?	

$\mathcal{R}$EVEAL

Now that you've connected with these women of the Bible, it's time to look at how God reveals His character and faithfulness through the relationship of Naomi and Ruth and how God is doing the same for you.

Where did you most see God show up in Naomi's and Ruth's lives?	
What does God reveal about Himself and His character in the lives of Naomi and Ruth?	
Like Naomi and Ruth, how have you experienced God's protection and provision?	
Where is God calling you to take a risky, radical step of obedience?	

$\mathcal{P}$RAY

Take a few minutes to ask the Holy Spirit to guide you as you respond to the following prayer prompts.

Lord, like Naomi, help me . . .

_____

_____

_____

Lord, like Ruth, help me . . .

_____

_____

_____

Lord, to whom are You calling me to be a second-mother or second-daughter?

_____

_____

_____

Lord, whom are You calling me to adopt spiritually just as You've adopted me?

_____

_____

_____

Lord, considering the story of Naomi and Ruth, how are You calling me to live differently?

_____

_____

_____

ELIZABETH AND MARY

Elizabeth was the biological mother to John the Baptist and a spiritual mother to Mary, and Mary was mother to Jesus. They model for us the very specific way God can place spiritual encouragers in our lives when we need them most, whether we are linked by blood or by heaven.

—From *The Mothers and Daughters of the Bible Speak*,
page 57

*M*ary and Elizabeth are cousins rather than mother and daughter, though Elizabeth is much older than Mary. God, in His wisdom, linked them beyond familial ties or direct bloodline. Both had miraculous paths to motherhood. Both gave birth to men around the same time who would change the world forever. God prepares divine journeys for each of them and provides their companionship as a gift.

*R*EFLECT

Luke is the only Gospel that gives us a behind-the-scenes look at the birth of John the Baptist, the forerunner of Jesus Christ. It's worth noting that God had been silent for about four hundred years. Elizabeth and Zechariah, along with all of God's people, had been waiting on God to break the silence and for God's long-awaited promise for the Messiah to be fulfilled.

Read Luke 1:5–7. How are Elizabeth and her husband, Zechariah, introduced in Scripture?

Much like the great wait of God's people for a Messiah, for what have Elizabeth and Zechariah been waiting?

What's something in your life for which you've been waiting on God?

How are you handling the great wait? What's helping you most?

With thousands of priests, it was possible to go a lifetime without ever being chosen to carry out this special task in the temple. When Zechariah is selected, he has an unforgettable encounter with an angel of God who echoes the long-awaited promise of Malachi.

Read Malachi 4:5–6. What is the prophesy in Malachi?

Read Luke 1:8–22. How will Elizabeth and Zechariah's son fulfill this prophesy, according to the angel?

Which of the following words best describes how you would feel before the angel Gabriel? Circle each that applies.

Excited	Angry	Joyful	Confused	Anxious	Hopeful
Fearful	Irked	Sorrowful	Leery	Eager	Worried

Which of the following best describes Zechariah's response? Circle each that applies.

Cooperative	Questioning	Doubtful	Brave	Willing
Worried	Surprised	Fearful	Whiny	Hesitant

In what ways do you think Zechariah's silence until the child's birth made him more attune to God during Elizabeth's pregnancy?

God works during the decades of delay in Elizabeth's pregnancy to script the perfect story to bring John the Baptist as the forerunner of Jesus into the world.

Read Luke 1:22–25. How does Elizabeth respond?

When have you seen delays in your life that are actually God scripting a better story for you?

Where are you struggling to trust God with His greater plans and perfect timing for your life?

How does Elizabeth's story challenge and encourage you?

Six months into Elizabeth's pregnancy, the same angel, Gabriel, visits Mary, too.

Read Luke 1:26–34. What does Mary's response to the angel Gabriel have in common with Zechariah's? How do their responses differ?

Read Luke 1:35–40. What does the angel Gabriel reveal about Elizabeth?

Why do you think God wants Mary to know this?

What does this reveal about God's desire for you not to walk alone during your times of uncertainty and need?

What is Mary's response to Elizabeth's news?

In your current areas of struggle, pain, or celebration, with whom do you need to reach out or spend time? What's stopping you?

> *B*ecause Elizabeth was filled with the Holy Spirit here, this was an act of prophecy on her part. She had no prior knowledge that Mary was pregnant, and no way of knowing. Elizabeth's proclamation had to give Mary added comfort, knowing that someone she already trusted and loved fully accepted the divine nature of her pregnancy. God knew well in advance that young Mary would be encouraged by mature Elizabeth's embrace of her situation, without question or doubt.
>
> —From *The Mothers and Daughters of the Bible Speak*, page 66

Read Luke 1:39–45. Who is the first person to call Jesus "Lord"? (Hint: v. 43)

How does God compel Elizabeth to celebrate Mary?

When you see women who share a similar success or joy as you, do you tend to celebrate them or compete with them? Explain.

The older, wiser Elizabeth becomes a source of comfort, a guide, and encourager to Mary. She's a spiritual mother to Mary. Like in this story, spiritual mothers share in our joys and sorrows, and—most importantly—help us understand those unexpected twists and turns in light of our faith.

They can guide us as we dig in and try to understand how God is working. That's especially helpful when sorrow, pain, or confusion enter our journey. And when we are filled with joy, they are there to share in it—just as Elizabeth and Mary did all those centuries ago.

Who has become a comforter, guide, or encourager to you through various seasons in your life?

When was the last time you reached out and thanked that person? What's stopping you from reaching out now?

To whom have you become a source of comfort, guide, or encourager during a specific season of life?

What's stopping you from reaching out and renewing that relationship now?

Read Luke 1:46–55. What does Mary say God has done for her?

The joy of this reunion between cousins and great news is too much to contain. Mary bursts out in a song of praise called the *Magnificat*, meaning "magnifies".

Which of these has God also done for her older cousin, Elizabeth?

Who in your life speaks the truth of God's Word over you?

Read Luke 1:56. What do you imagine Mary and Elizabeth talked about and bonded over during this time?

The love of two cousins who became a spiritual mother and daughter to each other not only framed the lives of Elizabeth and Mary, but also provided the actual human embodiment for the arrival of the gift of salvation for all humanity.

Where are you feeling most isolated or alone now?

What steps can you take to prayerfully find a spiritual mother or daughter with whom to journey through this season of life?

What can be the eternal impact of these relationships?

CONNECT

Now that you've read and reflected on much of Elizabeth and Mary's story, it's time to connect these women and their special relationship with your life. Fill out the chart below.

What do you see as Elizabeth's greatest character strengths as a spiritual mother?	
What do you see as Mary's greatest character strengths as a spiritual daughter?	
Which of these strengths do you relate to or long for in your relationships?	
How would you describe Elizabeth and Mary's relationship?	
How do you hope to be more like Elizabeth and Mary in your familial or spiritual relationships?	

REVEAL

Now that you've connected with these women of the Bible, it's time to look at how God pours His love to and through Elizabeth and Mary and how God is doing the same for you.

Where did you most see God show up in Elizabeth's and Mary's lives?	
What does God reveal about Himself and His character through the lives of Elizabeth and Mary?	
Like Elizabeth and Mary, how have you experienced God through a meaningful relationship at just the right time?	
How is God calling you to step out in faith and trust Him more with your relationships?	

$\mathcal{P}$RAY

Take a few minutes to ask the Holy Spirit to guide you as you respond to the following prayer prompts.

Lord, like Elizabeth, help me . . .

_____

_____

_____

Lord, like Mary, help me . . .

_____

_____

_____

Lord, who are You calling me to reach out to who is facing similar life circumstances or challenges?

_____

_____

_____

Lord, how can I best encourage this person?

_____

_____

_____

Lord, considering the story of Mary and Elizabeth, where are You calling me to trust You with Your perfect timing and greater plan?

_____

_____

_____

MOTHERS
AND
SONS

REBEKAH

*I*n journeying along with Rebekah, we see a life that started with incredible promise but veered into dangerous territory. Where were the off-ramps, the places where Rebekah could have corrected course? They were there, and by studying her, it's my hope that we'll see those opportunities for redemption in our stories.

—**From** *The Mothers and Daughters of the Bible Speak*, page 81

*R*ebekah gives us one of the most romantic love stories in the Bible. She's a bride chosen by God for Abraham's beloved son, Isaac. Yet when she becomes a mother, she allows favoritism to get the best of her. She assumes that for her son Jacob to get ahead, it's all up to her. Far too many of us are tempted to dabble with this path, instead of trusting in God's unwavering ability to accomplish what He's promised.

*R*EFLECT

As Abraham nears the end of his life, he focuses on God's promises regarding his lineage and becomes concerned with whom his son, Isaac, will marry. As a faithful servant, Abraham wants to ensure that his daughter-in-law comes from among his people, not from among those who serve foreign gods.

Read Genesis 24:1–9. What does Abraham instruct the servant to do and how does the servant respond?

Read Genesis 24:10–14. What does the servant pray and how does God respond?

Has there been a time you prayed and received an immediate answer to your prayer? Describe.

How did that experience strengthen your faith and what did you discover about God through it?

Read Genesis 24:15–27. What are the standout characteristics of Rebekah when she's introduced in the Bible?

What does she do that affirms to the servant that she's God's intended wife for Isaac?

When you pray, do you tend to make more general or specific requests of God?

How does the specificity of your prayer make it easier to see God's answer to the prayer?

Does anything hold you back from making highly-specific prayers? If so, describe.

The servant travels to Rebekah's house and tells the family his story, gives them gifts, and asks for permission for Rebekah to return home with him. Rather than waiting, she agrees to go right away.

Read Genesis 24:62–67. What do you suspect God did in the hearts of Rebekah and Isaac when they first saw each other?

> *J*ust like Abraham's son, Isaac, a bride was prepared for Christ the Son. We, the church, are the bride, and like Rebekah, we were bought with a high price. We were sought out and brought into a new family. We are treasured and lavished with love.
>
> —From *The Mothers and Daughters of the Bible Speak*, pages 86–87

This romantic story starts from such a beautiful place. Rebekah is from the prayed-for family line; she's hardworking, lovely, and trusts God's plan. She and her husband, Isaac, are head over heels for each other. Though she's barren for many years, Isaac continues to pray, and she becomes pregnant.

Read Genesis 25:22–23. What does God reveal about Rebekah's twin boys?

What do you think troubled Rebekah most about what God told her?

How has motherhood or spiritual motherhood not been what you expected?

How have you responded and handled it?

Read Genesis 25:24–27. Next to each name below, make a list of the distinguishing characteristics of each son.

   Esau:

   Jacob:

Read Genesis 25:28. What does this passage suggest about how Isaac and Rebekah turn to their children to fulfill their emotional needs rather than each other?

How have you seen family imbalance or favoritism impact you or those you love?

Jacob and Esau couldn't be more opposite. Their personalities, values, priorities, and goals differ greatly. But the first breaking point comes when Jacob exploits his brother.

Read Genesis 25:29–34. How does Esau allow his cravings to make a rash decision?

When have you allowed your cravings or desire for immediate gratification to get the best of you? Describe the circumstance and outcome.

What does it reveal about Rebekah and Isaac that they allowed their sons' rivalry to get to the point of no return?

Following the loss of Esau's birthright, the dueling sons' story pauses to refocus on Rebekah and Isaac. Much like Abraham and Sarah's perilous journey into a foreign land, Isaac and Rebekah find themselves living among the Philistines. Like Abraham, the king takes notice of Isaac's wife. Like Abraham, Isaac lies about being married to her. And like Abraham, Isaac must eventually move away.

But in the context of Isaac and Rebekah's story, there is evidence of how their relationship had changed since they experienced love at first sight.

Read Genesis 26:7–10. What does Isaac's treatment of Rebekah reveal about their relationship? In what context does he consider her?

How would you feel if someone had left you vulnerable for their own security?

As Isaac grows closer to the end of his life, Rebekah stirs the sibling pot of rivalry more. She's willing to do anything to ensure her beloved Jacob doesn't just get the birthright (guaranteeing a double portion of the inheritance), but also the coveted blessing of Isaac.

Read Genesis 27:1–17. What drives Rebekah to such manipulative conduct?

Why do you think she didn't trust God's promise that the older brother would serve the younger (Genesis 25:23)?

What promise of God are you doubting or second-guessing right now?

Where are you tempted to control or force life circumstances rather than trust God?

When have you been tempted to influence or engineer your loved ones' future? What was the outcome?

How does this story challenge you toward greater trust or resignation to God?

> Mothers have incredible sway over their children, but when they become obsessed with manipulating everything that stands in the way of the future they imagine for that child, no good can come from it.
>
> —From *The Mothers and Daughters of the Bible Speak*, page 96

Read Genesis 27:5–18. What characteristics does Rebekah display in this passage?

Read Genesis 27:41–45. What is the outcome or fruit of Rebekah's actions?

How do her actions backfire and destroy her relationship with her son and family?

What do you think Jacob and Esau's lives would have been like if they had not been shaped by parental favoritism and trickery?

Reflecting on your upbringing, from what do you most need to heal and break free?

Read Genesis 27:46. What is revealed about Rebekah's character that her last words in the Bible are a lie?

Describe a time where you once started strong spiritually but lost your way.

How did you, or might you now, repent or change your mind and set your heart fully and wholly on Christ again?

CONNECT

Now that you've read and reflected on Rebekah's story, it's time to connect this woman and her relationships with your life. Fill out the chart below.

What do you see as Rebekah's greatest character strengths as a mother?	
What do you see as Rebekah's greatest weaknesses as a mother?	
Which strengths do you relate to or long for?	
Which struggles do you relate to or long to overcome?	
What did you learn and want to put into practice from Rebekah's story?	

REVEAL

Now that you've connected with this woman of the Bible, it's time to look at how God reveals His faithfulness through the life of Rebekah.

Where did you most see God show up in Rebekah's life?	
What does God reveal about Himself and His character in the life of Rebekah?	
Like Rebekah, how have you experienced God working in beautiful, miraculous ways?	
How is God calling you to step out in faith and trust Him more?	

$\mathscr{P}$RAY

Take a few minutes to ask the Holy Spirit to guide you as you respond to the following prayer prompts.

Lord, like Rebekah, help me . . .

_____

_____

_____

Lord, considering Rebekah, help me not to fall into the traps of . . .

_____

_____

_____

Lord, toward whom am I turning in an unhealthy way to fulfill my emotional needs? Toward whom am I showing favoritism and causing harm?

_____

_____

_____

Lord, what's a situation where I'm trying to control the outcome, when I really need to trust You?

_____

_____

_____

Lord, considering the story of Rebekah, how are You calling me to live differently?

_____

_____

_____

ℬATHSHEBA

ℬathsheba, a woman so often disregarded (then and now) and one who endured excruciating loss, gave birth to the man who would bless God's people abundantly through his wisdom and kind rule. Not only that, but she was instrumental in making sure Solomon found his way to the throne.

—From *The Mothers and Daughters of the Bible Speak*, page 132

athsheba's story reaches all-time highs and brutal lows. She's summoned by the king for his pleasure, then sent home. She becomes pregnant with a child who isn't her husband's, then becomes a widow, then marries a king, and then loses the child. Joy bursts into her life with the arrival of her baby boy, Solomon. In a movie, this might be where the credits would roll, and they'd all live happily ever after. But for Bathsheba, this is the beginning of a new life, one that gives her a voice of power in the palace of David.

REFLECT

Just before we meet Bathsheba, a military wife, we discover something misaligned in the life of David. While other kings march alongside their troops (2 Samuel 11:1), King David hangs back and sends his army on without him. We'll never know why, but his absence suggests he was distracted as a leader. And this distraction soon entangles Bathsheba.

One evening, David strolls along the palace rooftop and eyes a stunning woman bathing. Bathsheba is busy fulfilling the scriptural duty of cleanliness and convinced she was safe from anyone's notice. But David eyes her and covets what he sees.

Read 2 Samuel 11:1–5. What does the Bible reveal about Bathsheba when she's first introduced?

What numerous decisions does King David make that result in Bathsheba's pregnancy?

What could King David have done to put on the brakes to his attraction toward her?

Is there anyone to whom you're inappropriately attracted right now? If so, how can you put healthy boundaries in place or discontinue the relationship?

What do you think Bathsheba felt and thought as a woman who could not refuse the king?

Now Uriah, whose name means "the Lord is my light," was one of the king's most trusted officers and loyal soldiers.

Read 2 Samuel 11:6–17. How does Uriah's faithfulness to King David compare to King David's faithfulness to Uriah, one of his chief warriors?

What does King David do to try to hide and disguise his sin?

How is Bathsheba impacted by David's sin?

David's commander, Joab, is forced to send his troops to undertake a risky and pointless action to disguise King David's murder. The king's actions result in multiple innocent casualties, including Uriah.

Read 2 Samuel 11:18–27. How does a man chosen and anointed by God become an adulterer and cold-blooded murderer?

In what areas has your heart become overgrown by sin? (Hint: envy, comparison, materialism, lust)

What warning does David's actions give you for the need to be honest and change before your desires lead you to action you will regret?

What do the following passages reveal about what God does for those who confess, repent, and turn back to Him?

Psalm 103:11–12

Proverbs 28:13

1 John 1:9

After David betrays Uriah, Bathsheba, and God, the prophet Nathan delivers a powerful story of injustice that evokes a passionate response from David.

Read 2 Samuel 12:1–6. What emotions does this story evoke in you?

Have you ever experienced anyone doing something like this to you? If so, describe.

Read 2 Samuel 12:7–9. What has God done for David and what has David done in response according to these verses?

David's repentance is immediate and profound. Nathan assured the king that his sin had been forgiven by God but warns David that God's punishment will be painful. The child conceived with Bathsheba will die. David clings to the mercy of God and weeps, mourns, fasts, and begs for the child to live.

Read 2 Samuel 12:10–22. How does David work through his grief?

How do you think Bathsheba responded to watching her child slowly die?

Grief is a good and healthy reaction to a fallen world. Our grief tells God that we cherish His gifts to us—we cherish them so much that we sometimes can't imagine our lives without them. Our pain tells God how much we value life. Too often mothers who lose their children—especially mothers who lose their babies before they are even born—feel they need to hide their anguish. I don't for a second think God asks that of us. Who better understands the grief of watching a child suffer and die than our own heavenly Father? He has suffered as we do, and He will meet us in our grief.

—From *The Mothers and Daughters of the Bible Speak*, page 119–120

In what ways has God met you in your grief?

Read Psalm 34:18. How have you experienced this in your life?

Read 2 Samuel 12:19–25. How does this encounter between David and Bathsheba differ from their first (2 Samuel 11:4–5)? In what ways does God redeem Bathsheba apart from redeeming David?

Bathsheba becomes the mother of Solomon, meaning peace. He is the oldest of David's sons. No longer a grieving young woman, she becomes a palace powerhouse. When we catch up with Bathsheba in 1 Kings 1, Adonijah, son of Haggith, is vying for the throne.

Read 1 Kings 1:11–22. What does the prophet Nathan advise?

What does Bathsheba risk her life to do?

How does Bathsheba, as a mother, act bravely and shrewdly in this passage?

Read 1 Kings 1:28–35. What is the result of Bathsheba's courage and wisdom?

Adonijah refuses to give up his grab for power. After David dies, Adonijah petitions Bathsheba to marry Abishag, a member of David's kingdom, not his own (1 Kings 2:13–18). Requesting possession of another king's harem was a power move. Bathsheba was no dummy.

Read 1 Kings 2:13–25.

Though Scripture doesn't tell us, perhaps Bathsheba knew exactly how Solomon would respond to Adonijah's request—making her happy to deliver it. With Bathsheba's insight into the plot of Adonijah, Solomon held onto his reign and sure defense of the Lord's will for the kingdom. For Bathsheba, who walked through devastating loss in the death of her first son, part of her reward was the joy of seeing Solomon seated on the throne. It's clear her son treasured her counsel and care. If you are a mother, you are constantly planting seeds of love and guidance—though you may sometimes wonder if you'll see the fruit of that this side of heaven.

Read 1 Kings 3:9–13. What does Solomon ask for and how does God respond?

Like Bathsheba, how might you plant seeds of love and abiding faith in your children and spiritual children?

Bathsheba, a woman who endured excruciating loss and betrayal, gave birth to, raised, and led the man who would bless God's people abundantly through his wisdom and kind rule as only a mother can.

How has your impression of Bathsheba changed after studying her story more in depth?

$\mathcal{C}$ONNECT

Now that you've read and reflected on much of Bathsheba's story, it's time to connect this woman with your life. Fill out the chart below.

What do you see as Bathsheba's greatest character strengths as a mother?	
What do you see as Bathsheba's greatest struggles as a mother?	
Which strength do you relate to or long for?	
Which struggle do you relate to or long to overcome?	
How do you hope to be more like Bathsheba in your familial or spiritual relationships?	

REVEAL

Now that you've connected with this woman of the Bible, it's time to look at how God reveals His presence to Bathsheba and how God is doing the same for you.

Where did you most see God show up throughout Bathsheba's life?	
What does God reveal about Himself and His character in the life of Bathsheba?	
Like Bathsheba, how have you experienced God's redemption after betrayal or loss?	
How is God calling you to positively influence those in your maternal care?	

𝒫RAY

Take a few minutes to ask the Holy Spirit to guide you as you respond to the following prayer prompts.

Lord, like Bathsheba, help me . . .

_____

_____

_____

Lord, like Bathsheba, what do I need to grieve and let go of?

_____

_____

_____

Lord, where are You calling me to be more courageous?

_____

_____

_____

Lord, where are You calling me to find my voice and speak up on Your behalf?

_____

_____

_____

Lord, in light of Bathsheba's story, how are You calling me to live differently?

_____

_____

_____

MARY, MOTHER OF JESUS

We most often focus on Mary around Christmas-time each year, as the radiant young mother overwhelmed by the miracle happening in her own body. But this is just the beginning of Mary's life as a mother. Along the way she would experience grief only a mother who has lost a child can understand, and before that ever happened, she would watch as her son was mocked, falsely accused, and rejected by the very people He was trying to save. As great as Mary's joy was at her son's birth, her sorrow later in His life was just as intense.

—From *The Mothers and Daughters of the Bible Speak,*
page 135–136

$\mathcal{M}$ary gives us a powerful portrait of deep faith and trust. Humbled by her assignment as an earthly vessel for the Savior, she rejoices in her calling—even though she knows many will never understand or believe the story. Mary's joy as a mother must have been immense, but hers was a story also marked by deep grief and sacrifice.

ℛEFLECT

According to the custom of Jewish law, a son is to be presented to the Lord forty days after his birth. Mary and Joseph arrive to dedicate their child, when two surprise guests, Simeon and Anna, recognize the boy for who He really is.

Read Luke 2:29–35. What do Simeon's words reveal about Jesus and His future?

What do you suspect Mary thought and felt hearing this?

Read Luke 2:36–38. How does Anna affirm that Jesus was no ordinary child?

Read Luke 2:39–40. What becomes of Jesus under Mary and Joseph's loving care?

The warning from Simeon was one of many Jesus' parents would receive. The last thing any parent wants to do is to snatch up their baby and run for their lives, but that's exactly what this couple had to do. The Magi, who visited the couple, are warned in a dream to return home by a different route and avoid King Herod at all costs. Then an angel appears to Joseph and instructs him to flee to Egypt to escape Herod's evil plan of terminating every baby boy under the age of two.

Read Matthew 2:13–18. What does the angel instruct Joseph to do?

How do the mother and father of Jesus respond to the instruction?

Take a moment to imagine yourself as Mary. The Lord of the universe entrusts you with His only Son, and now you're on the run, unable to give Him a permanent, safe place to call home. What kinds of emotions and thoughts would this stir for you?

As a mom or spiritual mom, what kinds of anxieties or worries are you wrestling with now?

In what ways does Mary demonstrate an abiding faith as a parent?

There are times when motherhood itself may feel like more of a burden than a joy—the endless (and frequently thankless) work of it, the exhaustion, the laundry, the cooking, the countless questions, and the micromanagement of running a household with small (and bigger!) children in it. Our faith doesn't require mothers to pretend that they don't feel overwhelmed at times. Motherhood will always be a mix of the highest highs and lowest lows, a reflection of our broader life in this fallen world. There is no Easter without Calvary, and every mother's journey will be marked by both delight and despair.

—From *The Mothers and Daughters of the Bible Speak*, page 136

Just as an angel in a dream instructs Joseph to run for their lives, after Herod's death, an angel in another dream tells Joseph it's safe to return to Israel. When we catch up with Joseph and Mary in Luke 2:41, we find Jesus fulfilling His earthly mission.

Read Luke 2:41–50. What do you think those days searching for Jesus were like for Mary?

What was most dreadful and terrifying for Mary in this passage?

What was surprising and joyful for Mary in this passage?

When have you been bewildered by God's mysterious plans?

Luke 2:51–52. How does Mary respond?

What have you been storing up in your heart regarding your loved ones?

This is the last glimpse we have of Jesus' childhood. The Scripture now transitions to Mary interacting with her adult son. Pause for a moment and consider all the years and experiences and memories Mary held in her heart from Jesus' childhood to adulthood. At the wedding in Cana, Mary urges Jesus to help with the short supply of wine.

Read John 2:1–10.

How does Mary demonstrate deference to God's ultimate plan and purposes? (Hint: v. 5)

Mary was blessed among women but was also asked as a mother to continually surrender her son and to watch. What grace and maturity did she model for us?

Are there any areas in which you're tempted to cling or smother rather than allow your child or spiritual child to take the lead? If so, what changes do you need to make to trust God rather than micromanage?

Read John 2:11–12. How does Mary's request and trust result in the start of Jesus' public ministry?

It's hard to imagine that as Jesus entered Jerusalem for the crucifixion that Mary was far away. As a loving mother, she likely watched the long walk of her bloody, beaten, beloved son. She stood at the foot of the cross. She watched as her son's hands were nailed to wood planks and He took His last breath. For those of you who are mothers, it isn't a question of *whether* you will walk through suffering in your motherhood; it's a question of *when*.

When have you felt helpless watching a child suffer?

What do you do when the path your child is on is no longer one you can rescue him or her from?

For mothers who suffer as they watch their grown children struggle to find their ways and choose things that will bring them pain, Mary has walked your path, too. The mother of Jesus lived all those things. Mary knew Jesus every day of His life.

How does Mary's story encourage you?

Mary keeps her eyes on Jesus. And this provides one of the most tender scenes in the Gospels. As Jesus is slowly dying in agony, Mary is right there. He shows concern for His precious mother and what will become of her once He is gone.

Read John 19:25–27. In what way does Jesus care for Mary as a son?

If Jesus demonstrates this tender care for Mary as His mother, what kind of loving care do you think He shows for you as a mother or spiritual mother?

After Jesus' resurrection, Mary again appears alongside the disciples.

Read Acts 1:12–14. What role does Mary play and what characteristics does she display?

or Mary, to be among excited and nervous new converts must have felt like the fruition of the hopes and dreams she had held in her heart for so long. Mothers devote themselves to a future that will outlive them, and they do so in the footsteps of Mary, who also worked for a promised expectation. They pray over their pregnant bellies, ask God for help through endless sleepless nights, and hope for a time when their children will embrace all the Lord has planned for their destinies.

—From *The Mothers and Daughters of the Bible Speak*, page 157

As a daughter, who are the mothers, mothers-in-law, or spiritual mothers with whom you've been blessed?

What characteristics do they have in common?

Who are one or two younger women into whom you can pour yourself?

CONNECT

Now that you've read and reflected on much of Mary's story, it's time to connect her story with your life. Fill out the chart below.

What do you see as Mary's greatest character strengths as Jesus' mother?	
What do you see as Mary's greatest struggles as Jesus' mother?	
Which strengths do you relate to or long for?	
Which struggles do you relate to or long to overcome?	
How do you hope to be more like Mary in your familial or spiritual relationships?	

ℛEVEAL

Now that you've connected with Jesus' mother in the Bible, it's time to look at how God guides and provides for Mary and how God is doing the same for you.

Where did you most see God show up in Mary's life and what does that reveal about God and how He wants to show up in your life?	
What does God reveal about Himself and His character in the life of Mary?	
Like Mary, how have you experienced God leading you through great heartache and celebration?	
How is God calling you to step out in faith and trust Him more?	

$\mathcal{P}$RAY

Take a few minutes to ask the Holy Spirit to guide you as you respond to the following prayer prompts.

Lord, like Mary, help me . . .

_____

_____

_____

Lord, like Mary, what are You asking for me to store up in my heart?

_____

_____

_____

Lord, what are the ways you are calling me into patient, abiding parenting?

_____

_____

_____

Lord, how am I clinging to my children and spiritual children rather than trusting You with them wholly and fully?

_____

_____

_____

Lord, considering the story of Mary, how are You calling me to live differently?

_____

_____

_____

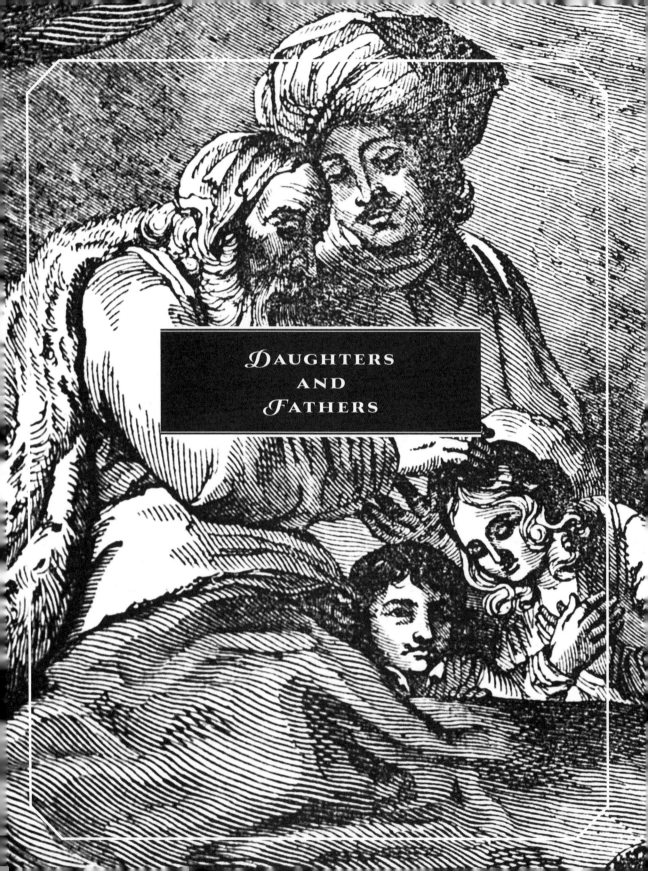

DAUGHTERS
AND
FATHERS

DINAH

*J*f we truly want to understand God's character and His plans, we can't skip over the stories that don't have happy endings. What we can do is learn from devastating mistakes and the consequences of purposeful disobedience and sin. The story of Jacob and Leah's daughter, Dinah, is one of those stories—full of horrible, broken people. One heinous decision piled on top of another until there was almost nothing left but a wasteland of violence and destruction, both emotional and physical.

—**From *The Mothers and Daughters of the Bible Speak*,
page 165**

Many stories in Genesis are tough to read. But it's important to delve into these parts of the Bible, as difficult as they may be. There are ugly sins to confront and hard truths to digest. Dinah gives us one of those stories and explores the influence a father can have over a daughter, and influence vengeance can have on a legacy.

REFLECT

Much like other stories we've read, when someone refuses God's instruction, it's a hint that things are about to unravel. God instructs Jacob to resettle in his native land (Genesis 31:13). Instead, Jacob and his family purchase land and settle outside the city of Shechem—far from the land God had directed him toward. Thus, their family is living where they're seen as outsiders, and where young women could be seen as fair game by ungodly men. During this time, something horrific happens to Jacob and Leah's daughter, Dinah.

Read Genesis 34:1–2. How does Shechem view and treat Dinah?

What does this reveal about Shechem's character, motives, and desires?

Have you or a loved one experienced abuse—whether physical, emotional, or spiritual?

What has been most helpful to your or your loved one's healing?

How should the modern church minister to and treat victims of sexual abuse?

Any woman who has ever suffered sexual violence can understand the kind of suffering that Dinah went through. For many women, the psychological toll can be even more destructive than the physical one. To undergo the violation of our bodies at the most intimate level tears at the fabric of our being.

There can be enormous healing in turning to qualified, compassionate professionals to walk a victim through the trauma. A support network of trusted loved ones can also help a woman weather the flood of emotions, from anger to despair. God Himself promises to bind up our wounds, to be close to the brokenhearted, and save those "who are crushed in spirit" (Psalm 34:18). The process of recovery and forgiveness can be long and agonizing, but it is possible. Survivors themselves are often the most empathetic advocates, able to turn their tragedies into paths that guide others to wholeness.

—From *The Mothers and Daughters of the Bible Speak*, page 167

Read Genesis 34:3–4. What red flags appear in Shechem's response and the way he speaks to Dinah?

Some abusers and rapists will attempt to sweet-talk their victims, whether to cover their own misdeeds or to convince the victim that they in some way consented or provoked the attack. We're told nothing about how Dinah felt or responded, only her rapist's selfish demand that she must marry him.

Read Genesis 34:5. What does Jacob's lack of urgency and neglect as a father reveal about his character and care for Dinah?

How do you think Jacob's neglect made Dinah feel about her value and her rape?

Notice that in this Biblical story, no one questions whether the rape happened. Many survivors of sexual violence say that one of the crucial turning points that helps them get through the trauma is someone believing their story.

Dinah's family did not even need to have the conversation; their belief in her, and in Shechem's guilt, was absolute. They did not sit down to debate whether Dinah should have gone out visiting that day. The Bible does not comment on her behavior in any way at all. That was irrelevant to what happened to her: Shechem raped her.

Hamor, Shechem's father, a leader over the region, feels the best way to clean up his son's crime is by negotiating a marriage between his son and Dinah. When Dinah's brothers find out, they hatch a vengeful plan.

Read Genesis 34:6–7. How is the initial response of Dinah's brothers more righteous than Jacob's?

Read Genesis 34:8–12. What red flags appear in Shechem's request of Dinah, Jacob, and their family?

Read Genesis 34:13–24. What do Simeon and Levi propose as a solution?

If Jacob handled the situation better, do you think Dinah's brothers would have had to develop their own dark plot for revenge? Why or why not?

Circumcision is the mark of Abraham's covenant with God, a symbol of the commitment to live as His people. It's the physical reminder that God had created a nation out of His unblemished promises. The third day after the circumcision of an adult male tends to be the most painful. That's when Simeon and Levi plan their attack.

Read Genesis 34:25–29. How do Jacob's sons go beyond justice and into bloodthirsty rage and revenge?

Were Simeon and Levi justified in deceiving Shechem and his family? Why or why not?

Should Simeon and Levi have used the sign of God's covenant with his people, circumcision, to murder? Why or why not?

What does Jesus say about mercy in Matthew 18:21–35?

Rather than recoiling at the horror, Jacob is only concerned about how the killing spree will impact him.

Read Genesis 34:30–35:4. How do Simeon's and Levi's actions lead Jacob to repentance and obedience to God?

Jacob never forgets the actions of his two sons and holds a grudge against them for the rest of his life. At his death bed, he says he wants no association with them.

Read Genesis 49:1–2, 5–7. What consequences does Jacob give Simeon and Levi?

What eventually became of Simeon and Levi? As Moses was dying and blessing the tribes, he leaves out Simeon altogether (Deuteronomy 33). Joshua 19 tells us that Simeon's descendants were eventually given land, but it was inside the land apportioned to Judah's. Simeon's tribe continued to dwindle and was essentially subsumed into Judah's.

Levi's descendants are given no land of their own (Joshua 18:7) and go to Eleazar, the priest, to ask for somewhere to live. The Israelites agree to give them various towns in which to reside, but they're dispersed all throughout the nation. In Joshua 21:21, we learn one of the cities Levi's descendants settle in is Shechem, where this entire tragedy started. The brothers' disproportionate, vigilante justice cost them and their families for generations.

—From *The Mothers and Daughters of the Bible Speak*, page 180

When have you been most tempted to take revenge?

What happened?

For what are you most regretful or grateful in the way you responded?

Though Dinah is central to the story, it appears everyone else has control except her. She's the daughter of an ambivalent father who drifts from God and sister to vengeful brothers. She's a victim of an evil man's actions and becomes the central character in a dispute that leads to a massacre.

In her pain and suffering, she reminds us that when those around us let us down, the only true One we can turn to is God. When others leave, God remains ever present, full of compassion, and with us no matter what.

What do each of these passages reveal about God's character and faithfulness?

Proverbs 14:3

Psalm 86:15

Psalm 147:3

Luke 12:7

Philippians 4:6–7

Which passage is most meaningful to you now? Why?

CONNECT

Now that you've read and reflected on much of Dinah's story, it's time to connect this woman with your life. Fill out the chart below.

What do you see as Dinah's greatest strengths?	
What do you see as Dinah's greatest vulnerabilities?	
What part of Dinah's story really connected with you personally?	
What abusive situation have you encountered that you still long to overcome?	
How do you hope to be part of a family or build a spiritual family that's God-centered, kind, and compassionate?	

ℛEVEAL

Now that you've connected with this woman of the Bible, it's time to look at how God is working through your story.

Where did you most see God show up in Dinah's life?	
Like Dinah, how have you experienced God working through tragedy and pain?	
Like Dinah's brothers, where is God nudging you to forgive and let go of vengeance?	
How is God calling you to pursue justice in God-honoring ways?	

$\mathscr{P}$RAY

Take a few minutes to ask the Holy Spirit to guide you as you respond to the following prayer prompts.

Lord, as you loved Dinah in vulnerability, help me . . .

_____

_____

_____

Lord, in what areas has my understanding of my earthly father distorted my understanding of You as my heavenly Father?

_____

_____

_____

Lord, in what areas do I most need Your justice, mercy, and compassion to flow?

_____

_____

_____

Lord, to whom are You calling me to show mercy rather than vengeance?

_____

_____

_____

Lord, considering the story of Dinah and her dysfunctional family, how are You calling me to live differently?

_____

_____

_____

ESTHER

The book of Esther is unlike any other book of the Bible. It's a real-life story that's as captivating as a fairy tale: the journey of an ordinary peasant girl, whisked away to a palace to win the heart of the king. The story is not quite that simple and involves all sorts of grisly political and personal scheming, as well as ideas of marriage that are very different from our own. Esther is a love story. It's also about palace intrigue, and the miraculous rescue of God's people. But underlying all those things, it is a story first and foremost about family: Esther's family.

—From *The Mothers and Daughters of the Bible Speak*, 186

Esther and Mordecai are technically described as cousins. But Mordecai takes in Esther as his own daughter when her parents pass away. In the Bible, families of choice are never second best. Like the story of Naomi and Ruth, these "found families" are an important model of the love and grace of God through His adoption of us, and our choice of faithfulness to Him.

ℛEFLECT

The Bible celebrates "found family," the idea that people not related by blood can still form deep bonds of care and community. The book of Esther reveals the richness and blessing that can come from that kind of family.

Read Esther 2:5–11. How does Mordecai show his love and tender care to Esther?

How does Mordecai's presence encourage and strengthen Esther?

Who has been "found family" to you—someone not blood related but still shows tender care and love?

To whom is someone you've been "found family"?

In both instances, how have you demonstrated your love through action?

Read Esther 2:20. How does Esther's obedience to Mordecai reflect a lifelong pattern?

Esther's obedience to Mordecai's instructions stands in stark contrast to Queen Vashti's disobedience toward the king, who now searches for a new queen. Esther wins the beauty pageant and becomes the new queen. Though the life might seem posh and easy, Esther soon faced an impossible situation.

The trouble begins with Haman, the king's trusted counselor. When Mordecai refuses to bow to Haman because of his faith, Haman grows angry and vindictive.

Read Esther 3:5–11. What is Haman's diabolical plan?

How does Haman's plan demonstrate his hatred for the Jewish people?

Mordecai informs Esther of the murderous order and asks her to risk her life by going to the king uninvited to stop the massacre. Mordecai, Esther's "found family," reminds Esther of her duty to him and the entire Jewish community.

Esther experiences a profound conflict of obligation. She's not only compelled to obey Mordecai, but she is also obligated to respect the king.

Read Esther 4:12–14. What reality check does Mordecai give Esther?

When was the last time someone in your "found family" had an honest, loving conversation about a change you needed to make or something you needed to do?

How did you respond?

When was the last time you had an honest, loving conversation with a "found family" member?

What was the outcome?

Read Esther 4:15–17. How does Esther respond to Mordecai?

When you're facing an impossible situation, who are three people you turn to for strength, support, and prayer?

✿ _____

✿ _____

✿ _____

Who are three people who turn to you for strength, support, and prayer when they're facing an impossible situation?

✿ _____

✿ _____

✿ _____

> Not all fathers and daughters are biologically related—just as we are grafted into our spiritual relationship with God. But Mordecai chose Esther, just like God chose us. God could have simply given us life, like He did with the animals, the birds, the fish—but they are not sons and daughters of God. God has made a way for us: first in His adoption of the people of Israel as His own family, and then in the adoption of all of us through Christ's sacrifice.
>
> —From *The Mothers and Daughters of the Bible Speak*, page 199

Esther goes to the king's court knowing she can be executed for approaching the king without an invitation.

Read Esther 5:2–8. How does the king respond to Esther?

What does Esther cleverly ask?

While Haman dreams up a dastardly plan to destroy Mordecai, King Xerxes can't sleep. He remembers how Mordecai exposed an assassination attempt on his life and how Mordecai had never been honored for it. In a beautiful twist, Haman lays out a plan for how such a man should be honored, thinking this will happen to him. Yet Mordecai enjoys the prescribed honor. Soon after, Esther makes her plea.

Read Esther 7:1–10. How did God use the "found family" of Esther and Mordecai to usher in deliverance for His people?

Considering this story, how does Mordecai provide an ideal of an earthly father and a reflection of the heavenly Father?

Read Esther 10:3. Though he could have coasted, how does Mordecai choose to live?

What could it look like for you to live in the same way?

$\mathcal{C}$ONNECT

Now that you've read and reflected on much of Esther's story, it's time to connect this woman with your life. Fill out the chart below.

What do you see as Esther's greatest character strengths as a "daughter" to Mordecai?	
What do you see as Mordecai's greatest character strengths as a "father" to Esther?	
Like Esther, what's the riskiest thing God has asked you to do, and how did you respond?	
Like Esther, from whom do you seek wisdom and guidance when you're making big decisions?	
How do you hope to be more like Esther in your familial or spiritual relationships?	

REVEAL

Now that you've connected with this spiritual daughter of the Bible, it's time to look at how God reveals His character and faithfulness to Esther and how God is doing the same for you.

Where did you most see God show up in Esther's "found family"?	
What does God reveal about Himself and His character through Esther and her "found family"?	
Like Esther, how have you experienced God working through the relationships with those you love?	
How is God calling you to partner with those He's placed in your life in a new way?	

$\mathcal{P}$RAY

Take a few minutes to ask the Holy Spirit to guide you as you respond to the following prayer prompts.

Lord, like Esther, help me . . .

_____

_____

_____

Lord, who is the "found family" You've given me to and called me to create? How can I love, nurture, and support them more?

_____

_____

_____

Lord, what's an honest conversation someone has tried to have with me that I dismissed?

_____

_____

_____

Lord, what's an honest conversation You've nudged me to have but I've refused?

_____

_____

_____

Lord, considering the story of Esther and her "found family," how are You calling me to live differently?

_____

_____

_____

MICHAL

Michal was a woman who found herself torn between two kings, in the middle of a terrible family struggle between her father, King Saul, and her beloved husband, David. This daughter not only chose not to participate in her father's sin, but she also actually undermined his nefarious plans. Michal was forced to choose between loyalty to her father and the vows she had made to her husband, David.

—From *The Mothers and Daughters of the Bible Speak*, pages 211–212

*R*aised in the royal court, Michal probably witnessed not only David's exploits, but also her father's initial greatness and ensuing downward spiral. She likely knew what kind of man her father was—or rather, the kind of man that her father's jealousy of David had turned him into. What a terrible thing it must have been, to watch the descent of her noble father into madness and evil.

REFLECT

Through the prophet Samuel, an unlikely shepherd boy named David is selected by God as Israel's second king. One tiny issue: Saul still thought he was king, though he no longer had God's backing or guidance. Saul struggles with explosive emotions. One of the servants suggests a musician playing the harp might calm him. David is called into the court, and his worship sooths Saul. Soon after, David accepts the challenge to battle Goliath, and God provides the victory.

Read 1 Samuel 18:6–15. How does Saul turn against David?

What does this reveal about Saul's character and commitment to God?

Who is someone in your life whose success has kindled jealousy or suspicion in you?

What steps have you taken to forgive and celebrate that person instead?

Saul hatches a plan to offer his oldest daughter, Merab, to David in marriage if he would commit to fight on Saul's behalf. David refuses by responding that his family is too humble. That's when we're introduced to Michal.

Read 1 Samuel 18:20. How is Michal introduced in this passage?

> It's not surprising that she would have fallen in love with David. After all, as a princess of the royal court, she would have had a front-row seat to David's heroism when he took on Goliath. She would have been a witness to all his heroic exploits, and she would have lived alongside him at the court. David had become the close friend of her brother Jonathan, and he probably seemed like a member of the family already. He was a dashing, heroic young man who had saved her whole nation.
>
> —From *The Mothers and Daughters of the Bible Speak*, page 217

Once again, David says he's not worthy of Michal as his bride. Then Saul suggests David pay a dowry of one hundred Philistine foreskins. If David said no, he risked looking like a coward after his victory over Goliath. If he said yes, the odds were that he'd be killed in the battle with the Philistines. From Saul's perspective, it was a win-win situation.

Read 1 Samuel 18:21–30. How does David respond to Saul's request?

How does Saul's evil plan backfire? (Hint: vv. 28–29)

What does this story reveal about Saul's spiritual state that he'd treat his daughter as a pawn and kill the love of her life?

What do you think it was like for Michal to watch her father drift so far from God into sin and despair?

Read 1 Samuel 19:11–17. How does Michal risk her life to save her husband's?

What does this reveal about her character and her love of David?

How does Michal's response save both Saul and David and her position in the palace?

When have you experienced family conflict that stretched your loyalties?

How did you resolve it, or are you still managing it to keep the peace?

When next we hear of Michal, Saul has treated her marriage to David as though it did not exist. In fact, Saul marries her off to another man, "Paltiel son of Laish, who was from Gallim" (1 Samuel 25:44). Meanwhile, hiding in the wilderness, David marries Abigail, widow of the wealthy Nabal, as well as Ahinoam of Jezreel. Michal's love story with David appears to have ended—the husband of her dreams gone from the palace, collecting other wives, and no prospect of their reunion because her father had married her off to someone else.

—From *The Mothers and Daughters of the Bible Speak*, page 222

How do you imagine Michal feels when Saul upended her life again (1 Samuel 25:44)?

In what ways does Saul's selfishness end up impacting lives far beyond his own?

When have you experienced conflict tearing your family apart?

When have you felt the pressure to make sure everyone is getting along?

In what ways is that a beautiful gift?

How can that place an unfair emotional burden on you that results in internalizing others' conflicts?

Eventually, Michal's father, Saul, is killed. His son, Ish-Bosheth, ascends to the throne, propped up by Saul's cousin and general, Abner. But then David catches a break: Abner defects to David, and he agrees to swing the war in David's favor. For Abner to prove his intentions, David asks one thing of the general.

Read 2 Samuel 3:13–14. What does David ask for?

David's request was a shrewd one. If Abner was going to defect, he needed to show David that he meant it. He needed to show David that even if he wanted to, he could not go back to Ish-Bosheth. What would be one thing that would prove that? Taking Michal, Saul's "possession," from right under his son's nose and leading her back to David. Michal was clearly the emotional battleground on which this battle between David and Saul was fought. In the list of Saul's unjust actions, this shows us that maybe it was taking Michal away from him that rankled David the most. The stage seems set for a romantic and loving reunion between David and Michal.

Read 2 Samuel 3:15–16. How does Patiel respond to losing Michal?

How does Patiel's response to Michal mirror Michal's response to David earlier?

When have you offered love to someone who can't or won't love you in the way you desire?

Michal was returned to David, much like a pawn, as a sign of his final triumph over the house of Saul. The Bible doesn't say what she thought or felt, until a few years later.

Read 2 Samuel 6:12–19. How does David show his love for God?

How does Michal respond to watching David?

Read 2 Samuel 6:20–23. What toxic stew of resentment has been brewing in Michal's heart?

After facing the injustice of sacrificing so much to side with David, losing her father to madness and death, hearing of her brother Jonathan's destruction, and the house of Saul, do you think Michal's feelings were justified, deep, or complicated? Explain.

Scholars differ on why Michal was childless—whether it was because she and David were never intimate again as husband and wife, or whether God withheld children from her as some form of judgment. In any case, that childlessness meant no descendant of Saul could ever be heir to the throne of King David.

—From *The Mothers and Daughters of the Bible Speak*, page 231

When have you or someone you know been caught between loyalty to birth family and loyalty to their new family?

What helped bring healing to the situation?

Why is it so important to turn to God to keep your heart soft in these situations?

How can you prevent the seeds of bitterness from taking root when you've been treated badly?

CONNECT

Now that you've read and reflected on much of Michal's story, it's time to connect this woman with your life. Fill out the chart below.

What do you see as Michal's greatest character strengths in her relationships?	
What do you see as Michal's greatest weaknesses in her relationships?	
Which strengths do you relate to or long for?	
Which weakness do you relate to or long to overcome?	
How do you hope to be more like Michal in your familial or spiritual relationships?	

$\mathcal{R}$EVEAL

Now that you've connected with this woman of the Bible, it's time to look at how God reveals His character and faithfulness to Michal and how God is doing the same for you.

Where did you most see God show up in Michal's family?	
What does God reveal about Himself and His character through Michal's difficult life?	
How have you experienced God calling you to keep your heart soft toward difficult family members?	
How is God calling you to trust Him in family relationships that make no sense?	

$\mathscr{P}$RAY

Take a few minutes to ask the Holy Spirit to guide you as you respond to the following prayer prompts.

Lord, like Michal, help me . . .

_____

_____

Lord, where have I allowed the seeds of bitterness to take root in me from being treated badly?

_____

_____

Lord, how do I love the most difficult people in my family well?

_____

_____

Lord, what are the deep, complicated feelings I've buried about my family that You want to provide clarity, healing, and wholeness?

_____

_____

Lord, considering the story of Michal, how are You calling me to live differently?

_____

_____

_____

MIRACLES FOR MOTHERS ... AND DAUGHTERS, TOO

Some of the most beautiful, encouraging moments in the Bible come when we see God reach into the lives of people in the depths of their need. It's a picture that points us to the reality that He is still working in our lives all these centuries later. The stories take us into moments of grief and places where there seemed to be no hope—where we can watch as God delivers a miracle.

—From *The Mothers and Daughters of the Bible Speak*, page 236

God loves to show up in miraculous ways in our times of great need. We see this in the stories of two widows who are visited by two prophets in the Old Testament. And we watch again, in awe, as Jesus meets two of His beloved daughters in profound and beautiful ways.

REFLECT

Elijah and his protégé, Elisha, reveal God showing up for two widows in their time of need. The prophet Elijah appears on the scene when Israel struggles under the wicked leadership of Ahab and Queen Jezebel.

Read 1 Kings 16:29–33. How does King Ahab choose what God despises?

Read 1 Kings 17:1. What judgement does God give to Ahab through Elijah?

The lack of rain kicked off a severe water and food crisis throughout the land. God sends Elijah to Zarephath to meet a widow who will provide for him. At first glance, the command seems preposterous. Widows were the lowest socioeconomic class that have no one to provide for them.

Read 1 Kings 17:10–12. What does Elijah ask for and how does the widow respond?

What does the widow's response reveal about her emotional and physical state?

Read 1 Kings 17:13–14. What promise does Elijah make to this desperate mother?

When have you found yourself in a situation with extremely limited resources and God calls you to sacrificially give?

What was the result?

On a scale of one to ten, how much do you struggle to trust God's plans when you can't see the end result?

When have you found yourself in a similar situation, where your resources are limited, but God is calling you to act?

Read 1 Kings 17:15–16. What is the result of the widow's obedience?

Yet God's loving care and provision don't end there!

Read 1 Kings 17:17–24. What causes this mother to panic?

When have you panicked in the face of tragedy, even though you'd experienced God's provision and intervention?

How does God show His faithfulness to this mother?

What does this reveal about God's faithfulness to you in times of need?

Elijah's successor, Elisha, was also used by God to show mercy to a struggling mother.

Read 2 Kings 4:1–7. Why is this mother so desperate?

What does Elijah instruct and how does the woman respond?

How did this miracle provide a testimony of God to everyone in the community?

When have you seen someone's suffering turn into joy, their need into a solution, or their deficit into abundance?

How did this impact your faith?

When have you seen your suffering turn into joy, your need into a solution, or your deficit into abundance?

How did this impact your faith and those around you?

What do the following passages instruct about caring for widows in distress?

Exodus 22:22

Psalm 68:5

1 Timothy 5:3

James 1:27

Who is one mother or single mother you can reach out to today to help in her time of need?

The Gospels bring us stories of daughters who need miracles, too. One of the most emphatic requests comes from a worried father. This man, a synagogue leader, presses through the crowds and throws himself at Jesus' feet in desperation.

Read Mark 5:22–23. What does Jairus ask Jesus?

How does Jairus demonstrate humility, faith, and love for his daughter?

Read Mark 5:24–34. What interrupts and delays Jarius from bringing Jesus to his daughter?

What do you think Jarius thought and felt during the delay—knowing time was of the essence and his daughter was dying?

Just like Jarius, how did the woman with the issue of blood, express her desperation for Jesus' healing?

Reflecting on Mark 5:34, in what area do you most need Jesus to speak these words over you?

Read Mark 5:35–36. In what area of your life do you most need to reject fear and embrace faith?

Read Mark 5:37–40. If you were in the situation, would you have laughed in disbelief at Jesus or accepted His words? Explain.

How does Jesus respond to those who mocked or displayed disbelief?

Read Mark 5:41–43. What does it reveal about Jesus' heart for family that the girl's mother, father, and the disciples are allowed to stay?

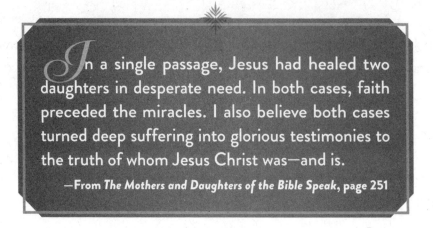

> *In a single passage, Jesus had healed two daughters in desperate need. In both cases, faith preceded the miracles. I also believe both cases turned deep suffering into glorious testimonies to the truth of whom Jesus Christ was—and is.*
>
> —From *The Mothers and Daughters of the Bible Speak*, page 251

What role does faith play in these two miracles?

When have you been tempted by scarcity thinking—the idea that there isn't enough blessing or healing for you and someone else?

How did Jesus' delayed response to a request for help result in serving a greater purpose?

CONNECT

Now that you've read and reflected on these miracles among mothers and daughters, it's time to connect these people with your life. Fill out the chart below.

What do you see as the greatest strengths of the widows and fathers fighting for their daughters' lives?	
What struggles in their relationships with God or their children do you see among them?	
Which strengths do you relate to or long for?	
Which struggles do you relate to or long to overcome?	
How do you hope to be more like the prophets, the widows, or fathers of these daughters in your familial or spiritual relationships?	

ℛEVEAL

Now that you've connected with these women of the Bible, it's time to look at how God reveals His character and faithfulness to them, and how God is doing the same for you.

Where did you most see God show up in these stories of great need?	
What does God reveal about Himself and His character through His response to those in need?	
Like these women, how have you experienced God working through your relationships with others when you've been in great need?	
How is God calling you to serve and love others who are in great need?	

$\mathcal{P}$RAY

Take a few minutes to ask the Holy Spirit to guide you as you respond to the following prayer prompts.

Lord, like these widows and daughters, help me . . .

_____

_____

_____

Lord, like those who fought on behalf of these widows and daughters, help me . . .

_____

_____

_____

Lord, who are You calling me to rally around through prayer, faith, and service?

_____

_____

_____

Lord, reflecting on all I've read in this study, what do You want me to know about You?

_____

_____

_____

Lord, considering all the stories of mothers and daughters, how are You specifically calling me to live differently?

_____

_____

_____

ABOUT THE AUTHOR

S hannon Bream is the author of the #1 New York Times bestsellers *The Women of the Bible Speak* and *The Mothers and Daughters of the Bible Speak*, the anchor of *Fox News @ Night*, and the chief legal correspondent for Fox News Channel. She has covered landmark cases at the Supreme Court and heated political campaigns and policy battles from the White House to Capitol Hill.

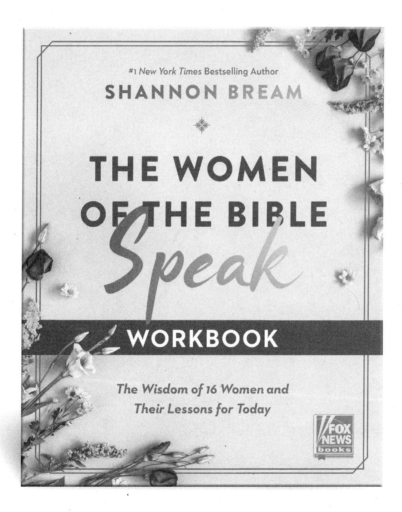

From the Publisher

GREAT STUDIES

ARE EVEN BETTER WHEN THEY'RE SHARED!

Help others find this study:

- Post a review at your favorite online bookseller.

- Post a picture on a social media account and share why you enjoyed it.

- Send a note to a friend who would also love it—or, better yet, go through it with them.

Thanks for helping others grow their faith!